TWISTS AND TURNS

By Nathan Lepora

Copyright © ticktock Entertainment Ltd 2008

First published in Great Britain in 2008 by ticktock Media Ltd,
2 Orchard Business Centre, North Farm Road, Tunbridge Wells, Kent, TN2 3XF

ticktock project editor: Sophie Furse
ticktock picture researcher: Lizzie Knowles
ticktock project designer: Hayley Terry
With thanks to: Carol Ryback, Justin Spain and Suzy Gazlay

ISBN 978 1 84696 614 9 pbk

Printed in China

Picture credits (t=top; b=bottom; c=centre; l=left; r=right):
Richard Bannister: 26. DreamWorld/Ride Trade Int.Corp.Est: 28. Rod Edwards/ Alamy: 9, OBCtr.
iStock: 22. Caroline Johnson/ Alamy: 4. Jupiter Images: 18/19 main. Kim Karpeles/ Alamy: 29b. Lake
County Museum/ Corbis: 19 inset. Mellor Images/ Alamy: 12. Photolibrary Group: 1. Joseph Rehanek:
25 inset. Howard Sayer/ Alamy: 20 inset. Shutterstock: OFC, 2, 6b, 17, 20/21 main, 23, OBCtr.
Illustrations by Justin Spain: 6, 10, 16, 21. Superstock: 14/15 main. Kumar Sriskandan/ Alamy: 27.
Illustrations by Hayley Terry: 14, 29. Trip/ Alamy: 5. David Wall/ Alamy: 7. WizData, inc./ Alamy: 3.
Colin Woodbridge/ Alamy: 13. www.coasterimage.com: 11. www.ultimaterollercoaster.com: 24/25 main.

Every effort has been made to trace copyright holders, and we apologise in advance for any omissions.
We would be pleased to insert the appropriate acknowledgments in any subsequent edition
of this publication.

CONTENTS

Rotation is movement in a circular motion. Roller coasters zoom around corners and swoop through loops. **Carousels** and big wheels spin around a central point. Their movements are examples of rotational motion.

TERRIFYING TURNS

Roller coaster tracks use twists, sharp corners, and loops to thrill riders. Roller coaster cars zoom from side to side, swoop up and drop down. The cars have **rotational movement** as they thunder through each terrifying turn.

SENSATIONAL SPINS

Carousels and flying swings act like giant spinning wheels. You sit on the outside edges of the wheel and rotate around its centre. As the wheel spins faster, rotational movement increases. The faster the spin, the more dizzy you feel.

LOOPY LOOPS

Loop-the-loops turn the cars upside down. As you roar through the loops, you whoosh up, flip over, and zoom back down again. Each loop, turn, or twist causes rotational movement.

For many riders the most thrilling moment is when they are upside down.

THAT'S AMAZING!

Inside your inner ear are tiny tubes filled with fluid. On a roller coaster ride, that fluid shifts and swirls, which makes you feel dizzy.

AXIS OF ROTATION

Imagine a rotating wheel. The wheel turns around a line, or **axle**, that runs through its centre. An axle provides a fixed line to turn around. It is called the **axis of rotation**. The wheel spins on this line.

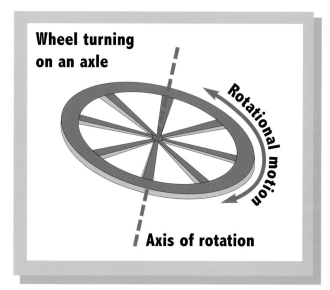

Wheel turning on an axle

Rotational motion

Axis of rotation

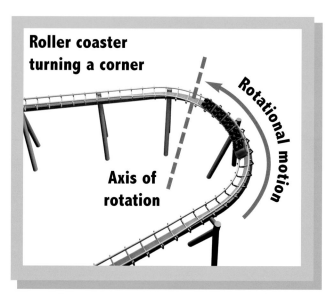

Roller coaster turning a corner

Rotational motion

Axis of rotation

A wheel turning and a roller coaster going around a curve are two examples of rotational motion. Both turn around an axis.

ROTATING ROLLER COASTERS

A looping or turning roller coaster car has a different axis of rotation on each turn. Each curving section of **track** is shaped like part of a circle. The car rotates around a central axis through the middle of each circle.

Axis of rotation

THAT'S AMAZING!

Even the spinning Earth has an axis of rotation. Earth's axis of rotation is an imaginary line that goes through the planet from the North Pole to the South Pole.

INVISIBLE AXES

Most of the time, you cannot see the axes of a roller coaster. Instead, the axes are the invisible turning points for that ride. Think of the axes as imaginary centres for each turn, twist, or loop-the-loop.

The axis of rotation on this corkscrew roller coaster points through the middle of the loops (towards the two distant trees).

Rotating objects have energy from turning or spinning around. This **rotational energy** is important for understanding how carousels, roller coasters, and swings work.

WHAT IS ROTATIONAL ENERGY?

Energy makes things work. Objects with lots of energy can zoom along very fast, burn with intense heat, or explode violently. An object without energy is unable to do anything.

Rotational energy is the energy an object has because it turns or spins. The faster an object turns, the more rotational energy it has.

THAT'S AMAZING!

Carousels were invented about 1,500 years ago for practising sword fighting while on horseback.

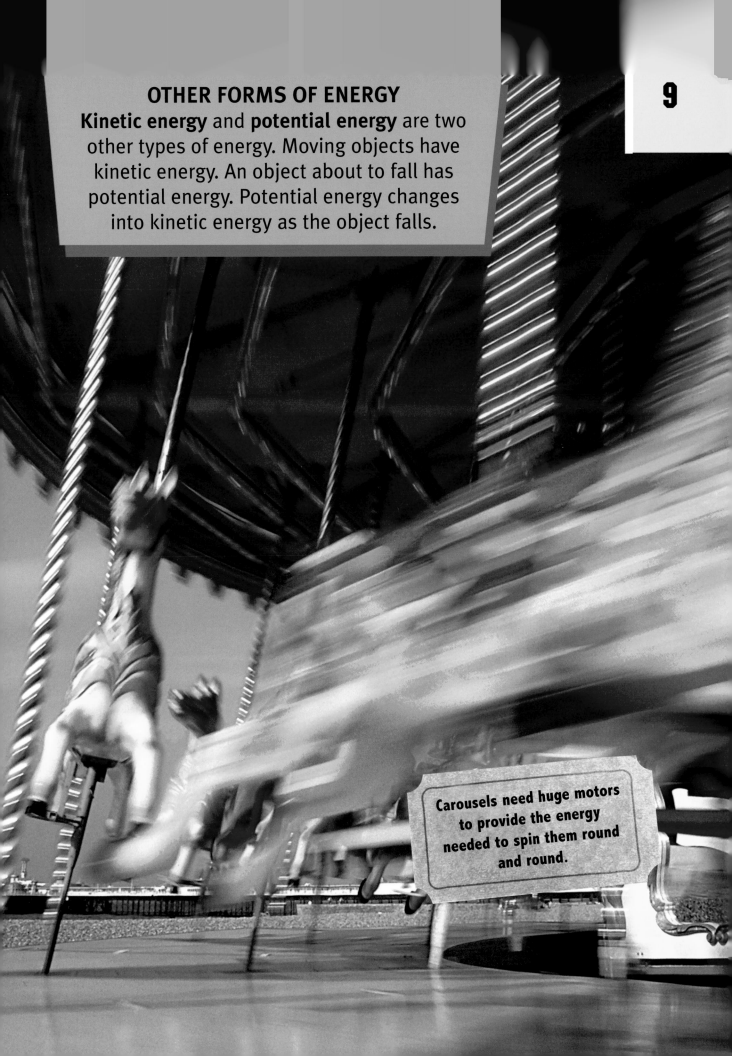

OTHER FORMS OF ENERGY

Kinetic energy and **potential energy** are two other types of energy. Moving objects have kinetic energy. An object about to fall has potential energy. Potential energy changes into kinetic energy as the object falls.

Carousels need huge motors to provide the energy needed to spin them round and round.

ROTATIONAL ENERGY OF A ROLLER COASTER

Rotational energy is similar to kinetic energy because both energies come from movement. However, kinetic energy causes movement only in a straight line. Rotational energy is produced by turning a corner or spinning around.

When a roller coaster car turns a corner, the kinetic energy becomes rotational energy. Before the corner, the car travels in a straight line because of kinetic energy. As the roller coaster car turns the corner, that kinetic energy changes into rotational energy.

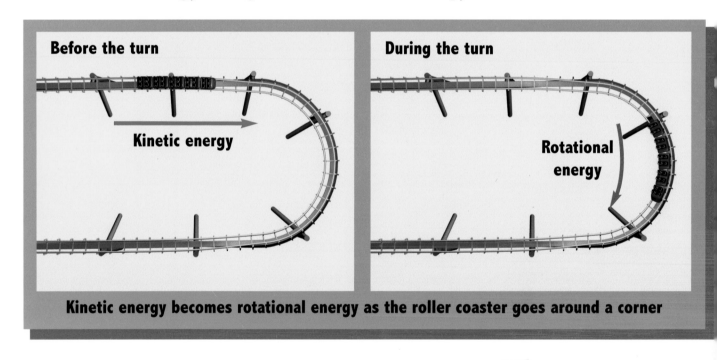

Before the turn

Kinetic energy

During the turn

Rotational energy

Kinetic energy becomes rotational energy as the roller coaster goes around a corner

DID YOU KNOW?

Most roller coasters are controlled by computers. They check the cars never get too close to each other. They also control the ride's speed.

ROTATIONAL ENERGY OF A SWING

As the **weight** on a **pendulum** swings, it also swaps potential energy with rotational energy. The weight begins to swing because of its potential energy. This energy becomes rotational energy during the swing. It then changes back to potential energy at either side of a swing.

A pendulum swing ride uses potential, kinetic and rotational energy.

When a roller coaster swerves around a corner you feel a sideways force pushing against you. This force causes you to turn with the car. It is called the **centripetal force**.

WHAT IS CENTRIPETAL FORCE?

Any object that is turning has a centripetal force acting on it. This force rotates a turning object through a corner, loop, or spin. Without this centripetal force, the object could only move in a straight line.

Centripetal force acting on a roller coaster comes from the tracks pushing on the cars.

Centripetal forces keep motorcycles on a wall of death

Every twist and turn makes the tracks push against the side of the wheels. This causes a sideways push that changes the car's direction.

Cars swerving through a bend push against their passengers too. Riders feel the push of these centripetal forces as the seat edges press against them.

DID YOU KNOW?

Centripetal forces act at a right angle to the direction of movement. As the roller coaster speeds forward through a turn, you feel strong sideways forces.

Nemesis at Alton Towers, UK allows riders' legs to swing free as they zoom around the twists and turns of the track.

TWISTS AND TURNS

HOW TO IMAGINE CENTRIPETAL FORCES

Imagine swinging a yo-yo around your head. As the yo-yo loops around, the pull of the string keeps it moving in a circle. A centripetal force pulls down the string to make the yo-yo rotate around the circle edge. Think of the string as the centripetal force in action.

If you let go of the string, the centripetal force disappears. Without the centripetal force, the yo-yo shoots off in a straight line.

Hand swinging a yo-yo

Rotational motion

Centripetal force

Axis of rotation

The centripetal force is along the chains holding the seats on this ride.

NO STRINGS ATTACHED

Now imagine an invisible string attached to a roller coaster car. Picture the car turning as it moves forward. Centripetal forces pull along this invisible string at every corner, twist, and turn.

Of course, roller coaster cars are not attached to strings. Instead, the curving tracks on the corners create the centripetal forces that pushes against the cars.

DID YOU KNOW?

Centri means 'centre' and **petal** means 'toward' in Latin. So a centripetal force pulls you 'towards the centre' of a turn.

Swerving around corners is exciting on a roller coaster. Corners can help you understand how centripetal forces work. On corners, centripetal forces pull riders from the outside edge of the track towards the inside.

CRAZY CORNERS

When a roller coaster car turns left, its axis of rotation is also on the left. The car rotates around this axis as it swerves through a corner. The axis of rotation is different in each corner.

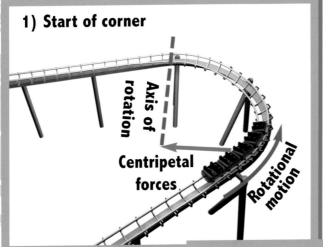

1) Start of corner

Axis of rotation

Centripetal forces

Rotational motion

Centripetal forces pull the cars towards the axis of rotation

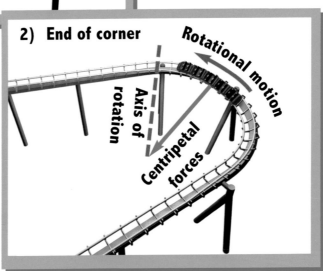

2) End of corner

Rotational motion

Axis of rotation

Centripetal forces

BANKED TRACKS

Roller coaster designers often build in a tilt or **'bank'** around a corner. The tracks are located at an angle to the axis of rotation. The centripetal force pushes into the tracks instead of across them. This keeps the sideways forces from pushing the cars off the tracks!

THAT'S AMAZING!

If you did not have safety bars on a roller coaster, turning a corner could throw you from the car!

The tracks on this roller coaster are tilted so that the cars will better turn the corner.

Loop-the-loops are fun because they flip you upside-down. Centripetal forces work with **gravity** to keep you in the car.

LOOP-THE-LOOPS

Loop-the-loops are simply vertical (up-and-down) corners. Rotational movement – sideways around a corner and vertically around a loop – propels you through the ride.

The tracks for a loop-the-loop propel cars upward at the bottom of the loop, and downward at the top. Centripetal forces pull the cars toward the loop-the-loop's axis of rotation.

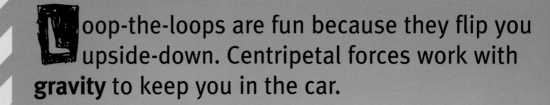

DID YOU KNOW?

Flip-flap at Coney Island, New York, was the first US roller coaster with a loop-the-loop. It was built in 1895, but closed in 1903 because of injuries to its riders. It is no longer standing.

Early loop-the-loops had a circular shape

Although they are very exciting, modern loop-the-loops are designed to be safe.

OLD AND MODERN LOOPS

Early loop-the-loops had a very circular shape. This design created strong centripetal forces that caused neck injuries by whipping riders' heads around too quickly.

Modern loop-the-loops have a special teardrop shape called a **clothoid** curve. The clothoid is a curving design that turns less tightly at its base to lessen the forces felt by riders.

HOW DO LOOP-THE-LOOPS WORK?

Gravity always pulls objects toward the ground. When you flip over an egg carton, the eggs fall out and splatter all over the floor. So why don't you fall out of a roller coaster?

The answer is good design! As you hurtle up the loop-the-loop, you are propelled up into the air. Then gravity starts to pull you down towards the ground. The roller coaster car loops around at the same speed as you are falling. This movement – plus your safety harness – keeps you inside your seat.

THAT'S AMAZING!

Colossus at Thorpe Park in Chertsey, England, holds the record for the most loops. It has a dizzying ten loops!

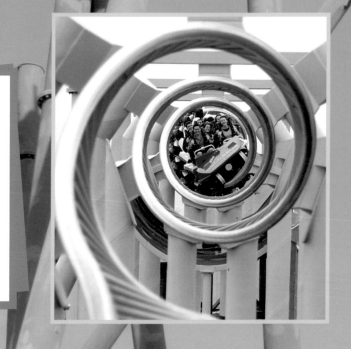

CENTRIPETAL FORCES AND GRAVITY

Gravity is the force that causes objects to fall. On a loop-the-loop you can also think of gravity supplying the centripetal force. Near the top of the loop, gravity provides the force that turns both you and the car around the loop!

At the start of a loop-the-loop the centripetal force points upwards. This force turns the car up towards the sky.

Start of loop-the-loop

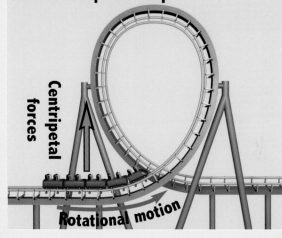

At the top of a loop-the-loop the centripetal force points down.

Top of loop-the-loop

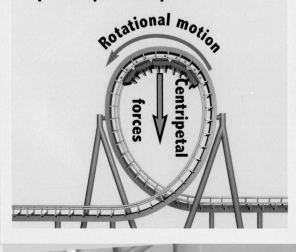

Theme parks have many spinning rides, such as **merry-go-rounds** (carousels), flying swings, and big wheels. Each of these spinning rides turn around an axis of rotation.

SPINNING RIDES

Unlike roller coasters, carousels and other spinning rides have a fixed axis of rotation. Riders whirl around one, stationary axis in a dizzying spin.

Riders enjoy the forces on a modern swing carousel ride

TURNING FORCES

Huge motors power spinning rides. These motors provide the turning force that makes the ride begin to spin (rotate). The ride keeps rotating until brakes slow it down.

Turning forces differ from centripetal forces. Centripetal forces pull toward the centre – the axis of rotation – to keep an object turning. Turning forces work along the outside edges of an object and change the speed of rotation.

THAT'S AMAZING!

The **London Eye** spins at 0.9 kilometres per hour which allows passengers to step on and off without the wheel needing to stop.

INTO THE FOURTH DIMENSION

Fourth-dimensional roller coasters are great fun. Riders sit on either side of the track in seats joined to long arms. The arms rotate freely during the ride to flip the seats forward or backward.

X at Six Flags Magic Mountain, California, USA was the world's first fourth-dimensional roller coaster. The ride starts with the seats tilting you headfirst down a twenty-storey drop. Then you hurtle through a dizzying series of twists, flips, and loops!

The fourth-dimensional roller coaster **X** at Six Flags Magic Mountain, California, USA.

SPINNING ROLLER COASTERS

Some roller coasters cars can spin while zooming along. A common type of spinning roller coaster is called a **crazy mouse**. The bottom of each car rolls along the tracks while its upper part spins around.

A crazy mouse roller coaster at Grand Island, New York, USA

THAT'S AMAZING!

The fourth-dimensional roller coaster **Eejanaika** in Fujiyoshida, Japan, flips its riders through 14 somersaults!

Another popular theme park ride has huge swings that whoosh forwards and back. The swings move with a kind of rotational movement. After each swoop of their flight, the direction of rotation changes.

SCREAMING SWINGS AND PIRATE SHIPS

A theme park swing ride is a large version of a children's swing. Swing riders sit in suspended seats. The ride makes the swings move up and down as they swoop in and out.

Pirate ship rides are another popular theme park ride. These rides feature one or two open-seated ships attached to a long arm. The arm swings back and forth from a **pivot** point, through which the axis of rotation passes.

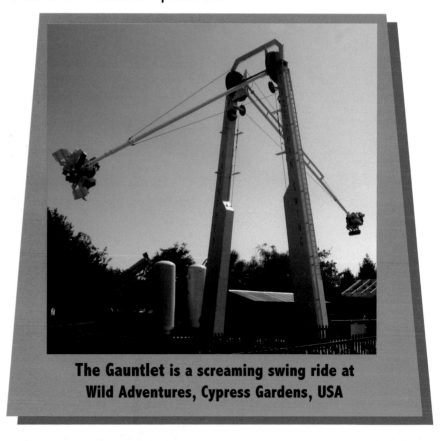

The Gauntlet is a screaming swing ride at Wild Adventures, Cypress Gardens, USA

WHAT IS A PENDULUM?

Swings and pirate rides act like giant pendulums. A pendulum is an object that hangs and swings freely from a pivot (a fixed turning point). If you pull a pendulum to one side and let it go, it swings back and forth until it runs out of energy.

The pirate ship ride, Santa Cruz Boardwalk, California, USA.

DID YOU KNOW?

The pirate ship ride was invented by Charles Albert Marshall of Oklahoma, USA, between 1893 and 1897. He originally called it **The Ocean Wave.**

HOW DO PENDULUMS WORK?

Imagine a simple pendulum consisting of a playground swing. As the swing moves back and forth, it travels along a curved path.

With each pendulum movement, the swing seat drops down, then rises back up. The seat passes through its lowest point in the middle of each swing. At the outside of each swing, it reaches the highest point.

DID YOU KNOW?

The length of the pendulum determines how far the pirate ship ride will swing. The size of the ship doesn't matter.

The Claw, in Dreamworld, Australia, is the most powerful pendulum on the planet. Here it is at its highest point.

The seat on the end of the pendulum moves because of gravity. As the swing seat falls, it accelerates (speeds up). At the bottom of the swing, it is moving the fastest. It is also moving sideways. The speed carries the seat back up in the opposite direction, ready for its next swing.

HOW IT WORKS

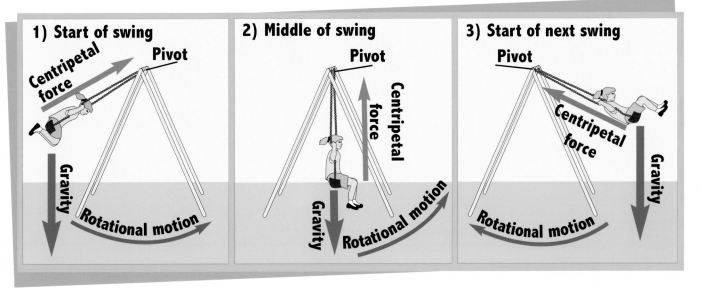

At the start of the swing, centripetal force pulls the swing seat in the direction of the pivot. At the same time gravity pulls it down. The swing seat drops down through the middle of its swing and rises back up again. It is then ready for centripetal force and gravity to pull it backwards on the next swing.

Acceleration is a change in speed as time passes. An object that is gaining speed is accelerating. An object whose speed is decreasing is decelerating.

Axle is the central rod around which a wheel turns.

Axis of rotation is the line along which an object rotates.

Banks are tilts along a roller coaster track or course that improve stability around corners.

Carousel is a theme park ride made from a rotating circular platform with wooden horses or benches for riders.
(see also merry-go-round)

Centripetal forces are the forces that pull an object toward the centre as it travels in a circle.

Clothoid is a teardrop shape used for loop-the-loops on roller coasters to reduce the centripetal forces felt by riders.

Crazy mouse is a type of roller coaster with small cars that spin around as they travel along the track.

Deceleration is a decrease in speed over time; the opposite of acceleration. *(see also acceleration)*

Energy is the ability to make something happen. There are many forms of energy.

Forces are pushes or pulls that change the shape, speed, or direction of an object.

Gravity is the force that pulls one mass toward another. Gravity also causes falling objects to accelerate as they fall.

Kinetic energy is a type of energy from movement.

Loop-the-loop is a section of a roller coaster ride that sends passengers looping up into the air, turning upside down, and looping back down again.

Merry-go-round is another name for carousel. *(see also carousel)*

Pendulum is an object hanging from a pivot that can rotate freely.

Pivot is a point around which an object turns.

Potential energy is a type of energy that is stored. (*see also energy*)

Rotational energy is energy from rotational (turning) movements.

Rotational movement is a movement that turns an object. Cornering and spinning are two types of rotational movement.

Speed is how fast an object moves.

Spinning is a type of rotational movement where an object turns around an axis of rotation that is centred within the object itself.

Swing is another name for pendulum. *(see also pendulum)*

Tracks are the rails that the wheels of roller coasters travel along.

Turning force is a force that causes an object to change its speed of rotation.

Weight is the pull of gravity on an object's mass.